WICCA

CANDLE MAGIC

A Beginner's Guide to Practicing Wiccan Candle Magic, with Simple Candle Spells

LISA CHAMBERLAIN

Wicca Candle Magic

Copyright © 2015 by Lisa Chamberlain.

Published by **Chamberlain Publications (Wicca Shorts)**

ISBN: 1508551405

ISBN-13: 978-1508551409

Disclaimer

No part of this publication may be reproduced or transmitted in any form or by any means, mechanical or electronic, including photocopying or recording, or by any information storage and retrieval system, or transmitted by email without permission in writing from the publisher.

While all attempts have been made to verify the information provided in this publication, neither the author nor the publisher assumes any responsibility for errors, omissions, or contrary interpretations of the subject matter herein.

This book is for entertainment purposes only. The views expressed are those of the author alone, and should not be taken as expert instruction or commands. The reader is responsible for his or her own actions.

Adherence to all applicable laws and regulations, including international, federal, state, and local governing professional licensing, business practices, advertising, and all other aspects of doing business in the US, Canada, or any other jurisdiction is the sole responsibility of the purchaser or reader.

Neither the author nor the publisher assumes any responsibility or liability whatsoever on the behalf of the purchaser or reader of these materials.

Any perceived slight of any individual or organization is purely unintentional.

YOUR FREE GIFT

Thank you for adding this book to your Wiccan library! To learn more, why not join Lisa's Wiccan community and get an exclusive, free spell book?

The book is a great starting point for anyone looking to try their hand at practicing magic. The ten beginner-friendly spells can help you to create a positive atmosphere within your home, protect yourself from negativity, and attract love, health, and prosperity.

Little Book of Spells is now available to read on your laptop, phone, tablet, Kindle or Nook device!

To download, simply visit the following link:

www.wiccaliving.com/bonus

GET THREE
FREE AUDIOBOOKS
FROM LISA CHAMBERLAIN

Did you know that all of Lisa's books are available in audiobook format? Best of all, you can get **three audiobooks completely free** as part of a 30-day trial with Audible.

Wicca Starter Kit contains three of Lisa's most popular books for beginning Wiccans, all in one convenient place. It's the best and easiest way to learn more about Wicca while also taking audiobooks for a spin! Simply visit:

www.wiccaliving.com/free-wiccan-audiobooks

Alternatively, *Spellbook Starter Kit* is the ideal option for building your magical repertoire using candle and color magic, crystals and mineral stones, and magical herbs. Three spellbooks —over 150 spells—are available in one free volume, here:

www.wiccaliving.com/free-spell-audiobooks

Audible members receive free audiobooks every month, as well as exclusive discounts. It's a great way to experiment and see if audiobook learning works for you.

If you're not satisfied, you can cancel anytime within the trial period. You won't be charged, and you can still keep your books!

CONTENTS

Introduction 10

Part One: The Wonder of Fire 12

Our Connection with Fire 13
Candles in Wiccan Ritual 15
Fire Magic 18
The Role of Color 22
The Next Step 28

Part Two: Preparing for Candle Magic 29

Candles for Spellwork 30
Choosing Candles 32
Being Practical 38
Consecrating Your Candles 41
    Clearing 42
    Charging 45
    Anointing 48
    Carving Symbols 51
    A Note on Timing 52
After the Work 54

Part Three: Candle Magic Spells 62

Getting Started 63

Love Spells..65

Moonlight Love Attraction Spell.................66

Finding Your Ideal Partner Spell................68

Spice Up Your Relationship Spell................70

Money Spells..72

Quick "Pocket Change" Money Spell............74

Rent and Bills Stability—7 Day Spell...........75

Banishing Money Blocks Spell..................77

Employment Spells...................................79

Lucky Job Search Spell..........................80

Employment Victory Spell.......................82

Healing Spells...84

Simple Healing Spell............................85

Healing Spell for Loved Ones..................87

Banishing Depression Spell.....................89

More Spells for Life Enhancement.................92

Courage Spell....................................93

Good Luck Spell..................................95

Helpful Answers Spell...........................97

Psychic Attack Reversal Spell..................99

A Witch's Craft.......................................101

Oils...102

Candles and Holders............................104

Conclusion.. 105

Tables of Correspondence..........................108

Table One: Herbs................................109

Table Two: Essential Oils.......................110

Table Three: Days of The Week 111
Suggestions for Further Reading 112
Three Free Audiobooks Promotion 113
More Books by Lisa Chamberlain 114
Free Gift Reminder 116

INTRODUCTION

Wiccans and other Witches have long known that candles are a great tool for transformative magic. Perhaps one of the oldest magical arts, candle magic is also regarded as the easiest and most simple form of magic for beginners to learn. This makes it the ideal starting point for anyone looking to start practicing Witchcraft.

It's important to clear a few things up before we get started.

Although this guide is primarily aimed at Wiccans, not all Wiccans consider themselves to be magical practitioners—some only use candles to revere the Goddess and the God in their many forms, as well as the Elements of Earth, Air, Fire, Water, and Spirit.

Furthermore, this book will still be of relevance to non-Wiccans—not all Witches consider themselves Wiccans, after all, and many practice magic without having a spiritual relationship with any deities.

Whoever you are, and whatever your beliefs, you are more than welcome here. However, it is worth pointing out that candle magic has Pagan roots--one trait found in just about any Pagan tradition is the belief in, and use of, the power of candles.

In this guide, you'll learn the basics of working with candles for magical purposes, including the reasons underlying successful magic, the best approaches to acquiring candles and preparing them for spellwork, and a selection of candle spells to try out on your own.

You'll also find ideas and resources for creating your own magic through the use of oils and herbs, as well as enhancing your work with an awareness of right timing by paying attention to the phases of the Moon and the days of the week.

However, no matter how much knowledge you acquire, it's really the practice of magic that leads to success. Be willing to try and try again, and you will ultimately find yourself with the ability to transform your life.

Blessed Be.

PART ONE

THE WONDER
OF FIRE

OUR CONNECTION WITH FIRE

Our earliest human ancestors lived for thousands of years before discovering how to create fire and harness its power—imagine how astounding this discovery must have been!

Perhaps because it's the only one of the four Elements that isn't automatically present in any given setting, fire has always had a magical, mystical quality to it. This can be seen in ancient myths, such as the Greek story of Prometheus, who stole fire from the gods and gave it to humankind in order to advance civilization. Similarly, in many Native American traditions, fire is also acquired rather than discovered, usually by animals with more power and ability than humans, who can't get it for themselves. Indeed, fire was seen in many cultures as a mysterious substance that wasn't simply made available to just anyone—it had to be acquired, often through the use of quick, clever thinking.

Our connection to fire has never really faded since those early days of our existence. Even today, despite all the innovative technology we use in heating our homes, illuminating our spaces, and powering our electronic devices, we still enjoy the primal quality of fire in the form of indoor hearths, outdoor bonfires, and, of course, candles. Gazing into the flames of a fire can be calming and meditative, a way to transcend ordinary reality and connect with the unseen forces that make the phenomenon of fire possible.

The ceremonial use of fire, in the form of candles, is found in most religions, including Judaism and Christianity as well as Buddhism and Hinduism.

But it could be argued that Wicca (and other forms of Paganism) is where fire really takes center stage, as it is used in a variety of ways and forms. Whether it's a bonfire for an outdoor ritual, a cauldron fire for making a magical brew, or a candle for honoring a deity, they all require fire. Candles are probably the most widely used "instruments" of the Element of Fire, whether they're instigating the transformation of reality, or simply lighting the ritual space.

CANDLES IN WICCAN RITUAL

One of the most fundamental uses for candles by traditional Wiccans, and many of their more eclectic fellow Witches, is to represent the Goddess and the God on the altar.

There are various systems of color associations for the deities. Gold and red are most commonly used to represent the God, while white and silver are for the Goddess, though some Wiccans use yellow and green, respectively. In traditions where the Goddess is emphasized as the central deity, she is often represented with three candles—white for her Maiden aspect, red for the Mother, and black for the Crone.

Candles may also be used to represent the four cardinal directions on the altar, with green or brown most commonly representing North, yellow for East, red for South, and blue for West. Alternatively, four candles may be identified with the four Elements of Earth, Air, Fire, and

Water, each of which is associated with one of the four directions.

Some Witches will also dedicate a candle to the "Fifth Element" of Spirit, often called *Akasha*, either in addition to or in place of the Goddess and God candles. The Spirit candle may be black, white, silver, or purple.

Some may also designate a candle for one or more specific deities they have a personal affinity or relationship with, such as a purple or white candle dedicated to the Greek goddess Athena, or a dark green candle for the Celtic god Cernnunos.

Like anything else in Wicca, there are traditions that follow as closely as possible the workings of Wicca's modern founders, and there are new, more individualized interpretations developed by later generations of followers. However you utilize candles on your altar, and whether or not you even have an altar, is completely up to you. My tip? Take the approach that resonates with you the most. If it feels comfortable and correct to you, it's the right approach for you to take.

When space permits, some covens and individual Witches like to mark the sacred circle with candles. This may be done with just four sturdy pillar or jar candles marking the cardinal points of the circle, or the circle's entire edge may be marked with tea lights. Using candles to mark the circle can enhance the atmosphere of ritual very powerfully, but it does require extra caution, and is not recommended for situations where small children or pets might come scampering by! Using tea lights in small paper bags weighted with sand or small pebbles is another option, and is particularly handy for outdoor rituals where breezes can make it difficult to keep candles lit.

Finally, candles are, of course, very often used in spellwork, both for purposes of ambient lighting and as part of the spell. There are elaborate spells, using many candles along with several other ingredients, and much less involved spells that may only require one simple white tea light. The spells in this guide have one or more candles as their central focus, although some will involve other fairly simple items like essential oils and dried herbs.

Before hurrying into spellwork, however, it's recommended that people new to the Craft spend some time learning about the theory of magic, particularly as it relates to fire, and to the use of candles.

FIRE MAGIC

Fire magic is associated with the functions of illumination, elimination, and transformation.

Fire literally sheds light, and can cause all but the most dense and solid matter to appear to vanish—though we know that really, the matter being burned is simply being transformed into something else which is unseen, leaving only ashes behind.

Fire can therefore be used in banishing work, whether you want to be rid of an annoying energetic attachment or a bad habit, as the energy of fire symbolically consumes what you want to eliminate. Many fire spells involve burning paper, on which you can write words or symbols representing what you wish to banish. As the paper is transformed by the fire, so the unwanted circumstances are removed from your sphere of influence.

The burning of herbs for purification of a space or a person's energy field is another form of elimination magic. Of course fire is also used to attract new energy and positive influences, and strengthen one's own courage and drive. Herbs or flowers may be burned for these purposes, as well as wishes written on paper—in this type of magic, the burning is a way of "sealing" the magical work of drawing toward you what you wish to attract.

The candle is a wonderful tool for working with fire magic. For one thing, it's much easier to work a spell with a single small candle than to build and start a bonfire! Aside from convenience, however, it's useful to note that candles are excellent symbols of the Elements, making it easy to represent each Element in a single object.

The solid base of the candle represents Earth, as does the wick, which provides the grounding mechanism for the flame to stay alive. As the wax melts, it emulates the shape-shifting qualities of Water, which can be found in solid, liquid, and gaseous forms. The smoke released from the burning wick evokes Air, one of the necessary ingredients for the fire to exist in the first place. And the flame itself, of course, quite literally represents Fire. So, as Elemental manifestations go, the candle is an excellent conduit for transformative magic.

But how does candle magic work?

Candle magic, like any other form of magic, works because of particular attributes of physical reality, both on the material (i.e. "visible") plane and the ethereal (i.e. "invisible") plane.

As we know from the physical sciences, all material things are made up of energy which is moving at varying rates, however slowly or imperceptibly to the human eye. Furthermore, all matter radiates energy, including matter that is undetectable by the unaided eye.

Candle magic is a way of harnessing the unseen energy of the Universe into particular thoughtforms that work to effect a change in the physical world—whether that change is tangible, like more money in your pocket, or intangible, like a more positive outlook on a situation that had seemed hopeless.

Thought, though invisible, is also energy—just look at how certain thoughts can effect emotional and physical changes in your body. In fact, it's really the power of thought that lies underneath both the simplest and the most complex forms of magic.

For a better understanding of how thought becomes an agent of change, it's helpful to take a look at one of the most commonly used sayings when discussing Witchcraft: "as above, so below; as below, so above."

This phrase is also known as the Hermetic Law of Correspondence, which states that whatever is true in the microcosm (i.e., the Earth) is true in the macrocosm (i.e., the Universe in total). Another way to say it is that the ethereal plane (also called the "higher" or "spiritual" plane) is a mirror of the seen, physical plane (also called the "lower" or "material" plane), and vice versa. In order to make a change on the material plane, magic works by changing the spiritual plane. The change then works its way through the linear time and physical space of the material plane until it is manifested.

If magic is the art of sending a particular thought into the spiritual plane to be manifested, candles make for particularly helpful "messengers." The request being made (also called the "intention") is sent through the medium of the flame, as the candle become the link between the Witch (or "microcosm") and the Universe (or "macrocosm"). As the candle burns, it disappears, leaving the material plane and joining the ethereal one, carrying with it the message of the intention.

It can take a while to get your head around this, but this is the essence of how magic works.

THE ROLE OF COLOR

In addition to the properties of Fire, literally embodied in the flame, the properties of color are a crucial driving force of the transformation in candle magic.

Color plays a major role in Wiccan ritual and magic of all sorts, and candle magic can be a good way to begin familiarizing yourself with the characteristics of color as they apply to magical manifestation.

For centuries, certain colors have been associated with certain intangible qualities or events, like love, luck, wealth, and death. It seems that red has always been associated with love and passion—the color of blood and therefore of the heart.

While "green" is a slang term for money in the United States due to the color of printed dollars, the color itself has long been associated with abundance in many parts of the world, due to the predominantly green colors of Earth during the growing season.

Wiccan systems assign magical properties and other associations to each color of the traditional "rainbow" or color spectrum, as well as many colors in between the primaries and secondaries. Lavender, for example, an "offshoot" of violet, can assist with challenges involving education, particularly in writing. Brown is associated with endurance and strength, and, as another Earth color, material abundance as well. Pink is associated with love, friendship, and emotions.

Some of these correlations may seem obvious from our experience of mainstream popular cultures, while others will be less so. What's more important than seemingly "logical" associations is the underlying physical properties of colors—how colors "work," and our role in the process.

This brings up another important Hermetic principle: the Law of Vibration, which states that *everything*, at the most basic level of subatomic existence, is in motion, or vibrating, at its own frequency.

Objects that appear solid and unmoving, such as houses or rocks, simply vibrate at a much lower frequency than the human eye can observe. The colors of these objects are essentially bands of light vibrating at different frequencies, which *are* observable by the human eye. Each frequency has particular characteristics suitable for specific purposes.

Another important point to remember about color is that it only becomes "color" when seen by the eye. It's the anatomy of the eye and its coordination with the brain that actually turns the light into a particular color.

In this sense, when used in magic, the color is truly serving as a connection between the self (microcosm) and the larger Universe (macrocosm). And because color also affects brain waves, can cause physical changes in the body, and can impact mood and behavior, it is an especially powerful force in the Universe to harness for magical purposes.

Combining the vibration of Fire with one or more particular colors, then, can and does produce changes in the material world, including in one's emotional life and in relationships.

For example, let's say you're having difficulty with a roommate, with whom you would like to get along with better.

You might work a spell with a blue candle, since blue, in magical tradition, is associated with peace and harmony in the home, as well as communication. Used in color therapy, blue has been shown to be soothing to the body, lowering the heart rate and regulating high body temperatures. It is also the color of the Element of Water, which is most often a soothing presence, such as in the form of a meditative indoor waterfall or the sound of ocean waves.

Between the physiological effects of looking at this color, and the message that blue sends to the spiritual realm, you have a potent tool for bringing about the change you seek. When you light the blue candle, you initiate the transformation by putting a physical force into motion that is received by, and then mirrored in the higher realms. This "mirroring" then causes the transformation to be completed on the material plane.

What will happen as a result of the spell? There is never an obvious outcome as the manifestation could take many forms.

Perhaps in a day or two, your roommate seeks you out for a heart-to-heart talk about the source of your disagreement. Or, perhaps it's you who finally feels calm and peaceful enough to initiate the reconciliation. Alternatively, your roommate may suddenly announce that he or she is moving out. The results of magical work can seem rather mundane or ordinary, or they may seem to come very unexpectedly—from "out of the blue."

If nothing at all happens for a long while, you may need to examine whether you are unnecessarily holding onto a grudge, or whether you had doubts about the spell while you were working it. Remember, thought is also matter—it's also vibration—and it has an impact on the degree to which your magic succeeds.

Below is a Table of Correspondence outlining some tried-and-true associations between colors and their magical properties.

Beginning Wiccans often find that working with widely known and widely shared associations strengthen the power of their intention setting during ritual. However, if there are personal associations for you between colors and meanings that differ from those provided here, it makes sense to go with what will help you focus the most.

Color	Qualities	Used in Magic for
Red	passion, courage, strength, intense emotions	love, physical energy, health, willpower
Orange	energy, attraction, vitality, stimulation	adaptability to sudden changes, encouragement, power
Yellow	intellect, inspiration, imagination, knowledge	communication, confidence, divination, study
Green	abundance, growth, wealth, renewal, balance	prosperity, employment, fertility, health, good luck
Blue	peace, truth, wisdom, protection, patience	healing, psychic ability, harmony in the home, understanding
Violet	spirituality, wisdom, devotion, peace, idealism	divination, enhancing nurturing qualities, balancing sensitivity
White	peace, innocence, illumination, purity	cleansing, clarity, establishing order, spiritual growth and understanding
Black	dignity, force, stability, patience	banishing and releasing negative energies, transformation, enlightenment
Silver	wisdom, psychic ability, intelligence, memory	spiritual development, psychic development, meditation, warding off negativity

Color	Qualities	Used in Magic for
Gold	inner strenth, self-realization, understanding, intuition	success, health, ambition, finances, good fortune, divination
Brown	endurance, solidity, grounding, strenth	balance, concentration, material gain, home, companion animals
Grey	stability, contemplation, neurtrality, reserve	complex decisions, binding negative influences, reaching compromise
Indigo	emotion, fluidity, inisight, expressiveness	meditation, clarity of purpose, spiritual healing, self-mastery
Pink	affection, friendship, companionship, spiritual healing	romance, spiritual awakening, partnerships, children's magic

Keep this chart handy as you choose candles for spellwork, as well as for simply improving the ambience of your home environment. After a while, you'll start to have an intuitive appreciation for the characteristics and "vibe" of each color, and eventually you'll be able to choose the most appropriate color for your work without having to consult any resources.

THE NEXT STEP

Before jumping straight into spellwork, it's important to prepare for it properly. This process involves choosing your candles wisely and getting them ready for magical work.

The next section provides a quick overview of the many different types of candles commercially available, and how to handle the candles you designate for magic, including clearing, charging, anointing, and carving them.

We'll also take a look at what happens *after* performing any kind of candle-related spellwork.

PART TWO

PREPARING FOR CANDLE MAGIC

CANDLES FOR SPELLWORK

For success in magic of any kind, it's very important to designate each of your tools for the purpose. This means making clear distinctions between candles you use simply for atmosphere, and candles you use for magic.

Don't work a spell using a candle that has already been lit for another purpose, even if it was only for atmosphere. While altar candles devoted to deities, Elements, and the like may be used repeatedly until they burn all the way down, candles at the center of the spellwork should be new, and consecrated for the purpose.

Often, candles used in spells are purchased specifically for the particular spell, though plenty of Witches keep themselves stocked in commonly required colors. Others might buy a bulk pack of tea lights and reserve a few for spellwork while using the rest for everyday atmosphere enhancement.

In fact, using candles for more than just ritual and spellwork is a good habit to get into.

If you can, keep one or more candles lit frequently while at home, particularly in the evenings, as these sources of natural light enhance the energetic charge of your environment, whether you're working focused magic or not. You can even direct that enhancement to help in a particular area of your life by choosing a specific color and location in your home, as we will see later on.

CHOOSING CANDLES

There are many different kinds of candles available these days—online, in gift shops, supermarkets, and specialty "New Age" and occult stores.

Some are more suited for single-use spellwork, while others are better for keeping on the altar, marking the circle, or simply lighting the sacred space. Some spells may require a specific type of candle, but most leave it up to you.

Tea lights are great for their versatility and portability. They come in their own tin or plastic bases, and so can be used in a variety of containers—votive jars, bowls, lantern holders, etc., or even just on a flat surface, without spilling melted wax.

Tea lights are most widely available in white, but you can get them in an increasing variety of colors as well. They can get very hot on the bottom—especially those in tin bases—so you do need to be careful about what you set them on, and you should wait several minutes after extinguishing them before touching the base. Bought in bulk, they can work out to be quite inexpensive and very nice to always have on hand.

Votive candles are similarly shaped but generally around twice the size of tea lights. They don't usually come in bases, so they require votive holders, which are often sold near the candles themselves in many stores. For those on a tight budget, votive holders, candlesticks, and even candles themselves can often be found at second-hand shops. If you don't want to use a votive holder, you'll need a plate or other flat surface under the candle, and you'll need to be okay with the wax melting all over the surface as it burns down. Some Witches embrace the "mess," making it part of the magical process and even divining messages from the Spirit world in the shapes of the melted wax.

Votives come in a variety of colors, and more than a few companies and "cottage" businesses now have lines of specially-designated votives for improving various aspects of daily life, such as prosperity, harmony in the home, or emotional well-being.

Tapers and other long candles require candlesticks, and may burn quite messily, depending on the type of wax and the strength of any air currents near the flame. However, a candle of this shape made of clean-melting wax and burned in a still space may leave very little dripped wax behind. Tip: If you end up with a holder too big for the base of the candle, you can melt a few drops of wax into it and then place the candle, holding it firmly into the wax as it cools and becomes solid again.

Pillar candles are much wider than tapers but still vertically oriented, and have less tendency to drip as they burn, though they also need to be placed on a safe flat surface, and depending on the candle, it may still be best to place a flat dish of some kind underneath it. In fact, it's always wise to avoid placing a new kind of candle on a surface you care about—such as directly on your altar or treasured furniture—until you know how the wax is going to behave once it starts to melt. For a guaranteed dripless melt, nothing beats a jar candle, which is particularly well-suited for repeated use. However, depending on the width of the top of the jar, these can eventually be difficult to relight as the wax level decreases.

Beeswax candles are becoming more widely available, and can often be found in many of the forms described above. While they tend to be more expensive than conventional wax candles, many believe them to add an extra special boost to their magic. This is due both to their lovely honey scent and the natural source of the wax—our friends the bees!

While many people may find it too extravagant to use beeswax candles exclusively, they are nice for special magical occasions and may be particularly powerful for spells working specifically with the Elements of Earth and Air.

Soy candles are also a nice alternative to conventional paraffin candles, as they are more naturally-sourced and result in better air quality.

Finally, there are what are usually referred to as "spell candles," which are small, taper-style candles, generally four inches in height and a half-inch in diameter, which are sold in many Wiccan and occult-oriented shops, as well as online. These are normally inexpensive, single-use candles in a variety of colors, each with its own properties and magical associations.

They require quite small holders which may be a bit more difficult to find than more "mainstream" sized tapers, but they can also burn fairly cleanly if well-balanced on a flat dish. (This should only be done when there is *zero* chance of the candle being disturbed and tipping over.) Many people find them to be very handy for spellwork, but if you can't find these particular candles in your area, don't worry. As always, it's the intention and energy you put into your spellwork that truly makes the magic happen.

Beyond size and shape, there are other considerations involved in choosing candles for magical use—the question of scent is a big one.

Some Wiccans and Witches prefer to work with scented candles, but they tend to do the "scenting" themselves with essential oils. Others find scents distracting and prefer plain wax. If you do go in for scented candles, look for those made with essential oils rather than synthetic fragrances, which have been found to be quite toxic to humans and bad for the environment. (Besides, you'll likely find, once you've worked with naturally-scented candles, that the artificial ones really smell horrible.)

The length of burning time is also something to think about, particularly for candles used in spells that are meant to be left to burn down on their own. If you don't want to be up half the night waiting for a candle to finish, look for those with relatively short burning times!

Candles meant to be in use through many rituals should ideally have longer burning times. There are some spells that involve 7-day candles, which are pillar-shaped and contained in glass, like the devotional candles used to honor saints. These can be left burning in a safe place for the full week of the spell. However, the general rule is to never leave a burning candle unattended. Even the most conscientious of people can accidentally cause a terrible fire, so it's always better to be safe than sorry!

As mentioned earlier, some candles on the market have been pre-dedicated or pre-charged for specific magical purposes. These are often wonderfully scented with natural essential oils, and can be used in meditation, as powerful energetic boosters of your magic, or as the central focus of a spell.

Some practitioners of the Craft are skeptical of the "store bought" factor of these candles and prefer to begin with a "blank" or uncharged candle, while others really enjoy working with them.

They can be particularly handy for beginners, though, as they can lend a little "extra spark" to those just learning to work with their own inner power. However, even if you do work with a predesignated candle, you should still charge it with your own energy before using it for magic.

BEING PRACTICAL

Some who are new to the Craft may wonder whether a candle purchased from a Wiccan store or occult website is going to be more powerful than one purchased at a grocery or department store.

The truth is that if you believe this to be the case, then it very likely will be so—and it is quite nice to get a candle from a source that respects the Old Religion and makes its goods available specifically for the purpose.

However, not everyone has the luxury of walking into their local Witch shop and stocking up on magical goods, and waiting for shipping from an online source isn't always an option. Plus for those on a tight budget, it may have to be candles from the big-box store, or no candles at all.

Whichever candles you end up with, there's no need to worry: you can always, always charge your "ordinary" candles to be just as delightfully magical as anything you'd find in a specialty shop.

Then there's the problem of not having the right candle(s) on hand for a particular spell or magical purpose.

Perhaps you're dealing with a breakup and having a hard night of it. You want to do some focused work for emotional healing, but find yourself fresh out of pink candles. You don't *have* to rush out to the store or order a special healing candle online (though you can do this if you prefer). You can use what you have on hand, including, and especially, your own creativity and intention.

For example, maybe you have a white, unscented tea light and some herbal teas in your kitchen. Find some chamomile and/or valerian to sprinkle around the wick. Maybe you have some dried wildflower petals, or are able to pick a flower or two from somewhere in your neighborhood. Do some freewriting about how you're feeling, and release the energy of these emotions into the Universe. You might tear the paper you've written on into pieces, and burn them. Then work to draw healing energy into your being. You can, and should, create your own spells, once you're comfortable doing so.

It can also be useful to consider letting what you have on hand guide the intention and direction of your work, based on what you know to be the magical properties of the color of the candle(s) and any other ingredients you know will be useful.

This kind of improvisation is easier once you've been learning and practicing for a while, but it can provide opportunities to go down unexpected paths, perhaps discovering that you have a particular need you weren't consciously aware of.

For example, say you want to do a spell for prosperity, but lack most or all of what the spells you're consulting require. Looking around, you find that you do have a violet or indigo candle, which are more associated with matters of emotional and spiritual insight.

Consider the possibility that the Universe is telling you that there are other issues to work on in order to be truly ready for the kind of prosperity you seek!

CONSECRATING YOUR CANDLES

Like any other tool used in magic, candles are far, far more effective if they are specifically prepared for use in ritual. The physical thought energy of your intention will find a clearer path to the spiritual realm if the physical candle itself is primed for magic.

There are many different ways to go about energetically preparing your candle. Terms for the process, and the number of steps in the process, will depend on the tradition of each practitioner, but the objective is essentially the same. Often called "consecrating," this is usually at least a two-step process, though some Wiccans add a third, which will be detailed below.

CLEARING

Most people will first clear (or "cleanse") their candles of any residual energy. This could be energy left from a prior owner or even someone who gave you the candle as a gift. It could also be energy from the manufacturing process itself, or the store where the candle was purchased.

Cleansing the old energy, or "psychic debris" from magical tools is done on a deeper level than just physically removing dust or dirt, although that may be necessary as a first step. What's required here is a vibrational clearing away of any energetic imprints that may obstruct the path of the intention as it makes its way into the spiritual realm.

The terms "cleansing" and "clearing" are interchangeable in their end result, but they present slightly different analogies of the process.

"Cleansing" is very close to "cleaning" which may bring up images of scrubbing an object vigorously to remove something dirty or foul. To some, this term seems to assume the presence of at least a small amount of negative energy in the object.

"Clearing" suggests a somewhat gentler process, with a more neutral estimation of the remnants of energy to be removed. If you intend to host a gathering in your living room, you'll first get rid of any clutter that would be in the way or be a distraction for you or your guests. Clearing an object removes energetic clutter.

Taking this step creates more of an unobstructed opening for you to channel your own personal energy through the candle, and, if appropriate, to charge it specifically for particular kinds of work. This is strongly recommended not only for spell candles, but also for candles you use on the altar to honor deities or Elements, and even candles that simply serve to light the ritual area. Taking the time to clear all of your candles will really enhance the energy of the space and the work being done.

There are many, many methods of clearing objects used in magic, but not all are appropriate for every kind of object. For example, athames can be cleansed by passing the blade through a candle flame, but this obviously isn't ideal for a candle itself, as you're just going to start melting the wax before the spell.

Gentler ways to remove old energy include burying the candle in a bowl of salt and leaving it overnight, or laying it out under moonlight. Both salt and moonlight eradicate the unwanted energetic residue, and moonlight has the added benefit of charging the candle as well. If you use salt, it's best to discard the salt afterward, as it will have physically absorbed the unwanted energy and won't be good for further use.

Alternatively, you can light sage or cedar and run the candle through the smoke to purify it. If you don't have sage, certain incenses with cleansing properties can also do the trick.

Candles that feel particularly in need of a stronger cleansing can be held under running water (except for the wick), or rubbed gently with a small amount of rubbing alcohol on a soft cloth. With either method, dry the candle with a clean cloth afterward.

Many Witches consider the clearing to be part of the preparation for a specific ritual or spell. Others like to clear their candles as soon as they acquire them—particularly if they hold any trace of stagnant or otherwise unpleasant energy. Do what feels right for you—which may vary from occasion to occasion—but it's advisable to refresh any objects that have been sitting around for a long time collecting dust, or stored among non-magical items, before using them.

If you're the type to stock up and save, wrapping your candles in tissue paper or cloth and keeping them with other magical tools is a nice way to keep them ready to use. You'll learn to sense whether a candle or other tool you've had on hand for a while could use some energetic sprucing up.

CHARGING

The next step, charging the candle, should happen closer to the spellwork if possible.

This is considered by many to be the act of consecration itself, while others make a distinction between consecrating and simply charging an object. There are several methods for this step, but all involve charging the candle with magical energy.

This step is a way to communicate to the spiritual plane that you are working to change some aspect of reality. Not every candle is necessarily going to be used directly in a spell, however, so the way you charge your candles may depend on how you plan to use them.

One of the more low-key and low-maintenance methods is to lay the candle on a cleansed, charged crystal for a day or two, or at the very least, overnight. As mentioned above, moonlight both cleanses and charges, and a Full Moon infuses objects with the strongest charge. Sunlight works as well, as long as it isn't too warm on the candle—you don't want the wax to start melting before the spellwork has even started!

These approaches are particularly good for atmospheric candles, and also work for altar candles representing deities or Elements. For spell candles, you might want to get a little more involved.

Hold the candle in your hands and focus on your goal. Visualize your positive personal power infusing the candle from the base to the wick. Sit quietly for a few moments with your eyes closed, feeling the energy of the candle come alive. If you're charging it well ahead of when you'll use it, place it on your altar until it's ritual time, or, for atmospheric candles, wherever it is in your home where you will burn them.

Words are a powerful tool of magic and most Witches consider them essential to the act of consecration. Chants, prayers, affirmations, etc. spoken aloud (or silently, if need be) help you focus your energy on the task at hand and communicate your specific intentions directly to the unseen world.

While Wiccans following particular traditions may have specific words they say every time they perform a consecration, others prefer to create their own blessings. You can use one of the following examples, or come up with your own verbalization of the transformation you're initiating.

Words of consecration generally state a connection between the person, the person's higher power, and the object being consecrated. For example, it's traditional to invoke the God and Goddess, as in this blessing:

Through the Universal power
of the Goddess and the God,
I consecrate this candle
as an instrument of magic.
Blessed Be.

Other Witches whose focus is less on deities and more on non-gendered entities of divine power may invoke the Elements, instead:

Earth, Air, Fire, and Water
come together in me
to charge this candle
with magical power
for the good of all
and harm to none.
So let it be.

When charging a candle for a specific goal, you can include the goal in your words. For example, you might say:

I charge this candle
through the Universal power
to bring good luck and health
to all in my household.
So let it be.

Whatever words you choose, you should be comfortable with what you're saying.

If the above examples feel overly formal or inauthentic to you in the moment of saying them, then the consecration is not likely to be successful. Forge your own path in transforming your candles into magical objects.

ANOINTING

Many practitioners add a third step, variously called "anointing" or "dressing" the candle with essential oil.

For some, this is not a third step, but is done at the time of consecrating with words as described above. Others rarely, if ever, use oil. But it you've charged your candle with magical energy without directing the energy to a specific purpose, oil is a great way to further prepare the candle for the particular spellwork you'll be doing.

Witches typically anoint just the spell candle itself, but some use oil on every candle involved in the ritual. As the heat of the candle releases the aromatic properties of the oil, the oil can greatly enhance the power of the spellwork, and in some cases may be the most important ingredient in a particular spell. However, the candle in itself still holds magical power, and oil is not strictly necessary for performing magic.

Like just about everything else in Wicca and Witchcraft, the use of oil is up to the individual's personal preference.

Essential oils are derived from plant matter—herbs, flowers, resins, and roots—and have both medicinal and magical properties. They have a variety of uses in the

Wiccan world: in ritual baths, as an alternative to incense, and as fragrance worn on the body, just to name a few.

Like candle colors, each type of oil has particular properties and magical associations, and can really enhance a candle-focused spell. For example, lavender oil is good for working to remove anxiety, and patchouli is associated with prosperity. Magical oil blends can increase the potency of a spell, so that you might add bergamot and cinnamon to the patchouli, as they add associations of success and luck. (You'll find a Table of Correspondence of common essential oils in the Appendix of this guide.)

Both single oils and pre-made magical blends can be found in metaphysical/occult shops as well as online, and recipes for homemade blends are widely available. Do follow instructions carefully—many oils are not safe to put directly on the skin without a carrier oil to dilute their strength, and none should be ingested.

If you're lacking access to essential oils or if they're out of your budget range (or if you're simply into a DIY style of magic), you can also fashion your own anointing oils by adding dried herbs to olive or sweet almond oil.

To anoint your candle, place one to three drops of oil on the fingertips of your dominant hand—also known as your "power hand." Use gloves if the oil isn't safe for skin, and use more or less oil according to the size of the candle. A small spell candle, for example, might only need one drop. Holding the candle in your other hand, rub the oil into it, being sure to choose the starting place, as well as the direction, deliberately, rather than simply spreading the oil all over the candle in a random fashion.

Most traditions hold that there are two different ways to anoint the candle, depending on whether your spellwork is for bringing something to you, or pushing something away. For example, you may be working to bring more prosperity into your life, or you may be working to banish a bad habit.

For attracting positive things, you can start at the top of the candle and rub the oil in a downward motion toward the middle. Stop there, and then work upward from the bottom of the candle toward the middle.

For banishing unwanted things, start in the middle and rub the oil upward to the top, then downward to the bottom.

Alternatively, you can rub the oil from top to bottom for attracting, and from bottom to top for banishing. You may wish to try both methods to see what feels right to you.

Consecrating and anointing your candle as close to the spellwork as possible is ideal, but caution is extremely important when working with oil, especially if you're anointing during the spell itself. Oil is flammable, so be very light with it if you're not going to leave it time to dry. Too much oil can cause the flame to burn too high, and/or overpower the wick, and there's risk of burning your fingers if you're not careful.

To really be on the safe side, you can use a cloth (consecrated for the purpose, of course!) as an intermediary between your fingers and the candle, or to wipe off any excess oil before handling a match or a lighter. If the oil is skin-safe, you can also dab leftover oil onto your pulse points for a strengthening of the magical connection between yourself and the candle.

For even further enhancement of your candle, you can roll the oiled base in crushed herbs that correspond with your magical goal. Dried rosemary can add a boost to a candle used in attracting love, for example. For those so inclined, a Table of Correspondence of herbs is also included at the end of this guide.

CARVING SYMBOLS

Lastly, etching a symbol or other message into the wax is a common element of candle magic. Runic symbols work well for this, as are other, modern-day representations, such as a peace sign in a spell to resolve an argument. If the work is on behalf of someone else, their initials might be used, and some Wiccans will carve symbols representing the Goddess and/or the God, some other deity, or one or more of the Elements.

In spellwork, the carving is usually done during the focused ritual itself, but some Witches may do it in advance, using the activity as a way of getting in the right mind frame for magic.

To carve a symbol you can use your athame, if you have one, or a reasonably sharp crystal point, or another, similar tool that has been cleared and charged for magical work. (Pins are popular choices.)

As you carve, visualize your magical goal, being sure to focus on the end result of the spellwork as if it has already manifested. If you're devoting the candle to a deity or Element, visualize the positive power of the divine energy surrounding you and working through you. This will enhance the connection with this energy when you light the candle during ritual.

A NOTE ON TIMING

It has been suggested above that charging and/or anointing your candle as close to the spellwork as possible is ideal.

However, depending on how elaborate you get with your magical work—particularly if you only practice within the larger context of a full Wiccan ritual—doing all the preparations right beforehand may be time-prohibitive.

We live in a busy world, and not everyone has more than an hour or so to devote to spellwork in a given day. Just as busy cooks might chop vegetables the night before preparing a meal, some Witches may out of necessity end up charging and consecrating their candles (or other tools) well ahead of the actual spellwork.

This is fine, but keep in mind that the energy used in *preparing* for ritual is just as much a part of magical work as *enacting* it. So if you don't have much time between the end of your day and the ritual itself, at least leave yourself a few moments to calm your mind and prepare to focus on magic.

AFTER THE WORK

In candle magic, as in any form of magic, the spellwork itself is what takes center stage. However, what happens after you gather your ingredients, speak your intentions, and light the candle is also important.

It's highly recommended that you close your magical ritual with as much focus and intention as you had while performing the work. Don't rush off right away to make a phone call or wash the dishes! Not only will you probably feel "out of sorts" from abruptly changing from one energetic state to another, but the magical intention may not get the right "send-off" to have an effect. Instead, spend some time in quiet reflection and commune with your candle. Allow yourself time to transition from the altered state of consciousness induced by magical work back into the mundane quality of everyday life. Acknowledge the changed energy in the space where the spell was worked, and thank the spirit world for its presence.

As you gain experience with this form of magic, you'll start to really appreciate the unique qualities of each and every candle.

No two candles burn exactly alike, which you will easily see by burning two seemingly identical candles at the same time. They will drip at different rates, and the flames will move in different ways. Some may crackle and hiss as they burn down while others may be quite silent. Remembering the Law of Vibration is appropriate here, as you witness the ever-present motion of Fire in a single flame.

Flames can make for excellent divinatory communication, as can the smoke they produce as it twists and curls up toward the sky. As you gaze into the flame, keep an eye out for any particular shapes seeming to come up from the wick. Is the flame leaning toward you? Away from you? Notice how it thins as it stretches upward and then widens as it drops back.

In some traditions, if the flame is high and strong, the work is proceeding quickly, while a low, weak flame indicates that not much spiritual energy is being invested in the cause.

It's also said that if the wick produces black or thick smoke, that there is active opposition to the work. This could be coming from a person, an unknown set of circumstances, or even the unconscious mind of the person working the spell.

Remember, however, that different kinds of candles burn differently, so it helps to get familiar with the way a certain kind burns before jumping to any conclusions based on how an individual candle burns.

When you're ready to close the ritual, you'll want to be sure that the candle is in a safe place to burn all the way down. Depending on its size, you might gently place it in a sink or a large ceramic bowl. If you have a cauldron, this can be an ideal place to leave it. Do be sure that there is nothing nearby that could catch fire if the candle were to somehow get knocked over! Because you may often be working candle spells at night, it's wise to use smaller, shorter candles that won't take several hours to burn all the way down. The spell candles mentioned above are very handy for this reason.

Not every candle needs to be left to burn out on its own. While this is highly recommended for most spell candles, other candles used in ritual—whether for atmosphere or for representing deities or Elements—are likely to be used several times before they're burned all the way down.

For extinguishing these candles, a candle snuffer is ideal, though it is certainly not necessary. Some Wiccans will wave their hands briskly back and forth over the flame until it goes out, though you need to be careful not to burn yourself! There is debate among different traditions over whether blowing out a candle is ever permitted. Some consider this to be disrespectful to the spirit of the Fire, while others believe that if you are sure to thank the Fire respectfully for lending its power to your work, then blowing it out, as gently as possible, is fine. And for what it's worth, both waving and blowing do tend to produce some great swirling images in the resulting smoke!

As with anything else in magic, listen to your inner voice when deciding how to extinguish your candles. Following someone else's instructions when you don't agree with them is not likely to result in successful results.

For some people, leaving a candle to burn out on its own may simply not be an option, whether due to time constraints, small children who get into everything no matter what, pets, or other reasons. Worrying about the possibility of injury or fire damage is likely to reduce the effectiveness of the spell, as is worrying about "ruining" the spell by extinguishing the candle.

Fortunately, there is an alternative approach to candle spell work that doesn't require a single, complete burn of the candle, but rather calls for a series of lightings over a span of days. In this method, the intention set during the first lighting is repeated each night of the spell, strengthening the overall power of the message being sent out into the Universe.

Depending on your goal, this may prove a better method than a single-night spell, and a few of the spells in the following section will make use of this method.

Once you've gotten more comfortable with spellwork, you can adjust the spells to your needs, by turning a single-night spell into a longer one, or vice versa. The more you personalize your magical work, the more powerful it is likely to be.

One really fun and interesting way to augment your magical work after a spell has been cast is to "read" any melted wax left behind.

Known as ceromancy, this form of divination doesn't tend to come easily to many beginners, but if you have any practice with scrying in water or a crystal ball, you should be able to adapt these skills to the shapes, forms, and patterns left by melted candle wax.

While some candles will burn fairly cleanly, so that little to no wax drippings remain, others will melt all over the place, providing opportunities to receive messages from the spirit world regarding the situation you've been working magic for. Some people will purposefully use votive candles on plates, rather than in candle holders, for this purpose. Many taper-style candles tend to drip profusely, so these can also be good to work with if you're wanting to experiment with ceromancy and don't mind a mess!

As you gaze over the melted wax, look for shapes and/or patterns that suggest anything about the forces taking shape around your request. In which direction did the air push the wax as it melted? What does the "mood" of the overall appearance of the wax seem to be?

Record your impressions in a journal or Book of Shadows, and return to them when more is known about the situation to see whether you were more or less correct. In this way, you can develop your own symbolic system of ceromancy and grow more adept at this form of divination as you continue to work with candle magic.

Finally, before you begin to experiment with magic, it's important to acknowledge the effects, and the process, of these time-honored forces of nature.

The old advice to "be careful what you wish for" comes into play here, as any work done with intention is going to have some kind of effect, and can often be unpredictable. This is why it's important to specify, when stating your intention, that the work be done "for the good of all, and with harm to none." You don't have to use this exact phrase, but the point is to state to the Universe that you do not want any ill effects to occur as a consequence of your intention being manifested in the material world.

To use a *very extreme* example, say you're working magic for a new job. A few days later, a cook at a nearby restaurant breaks an ankle and can't come to work for three months, so a job opens up and you get hired to take his place.

Now, it's arguable that this cook must have had his own karmic lessons to learn at this time, and that the injury and resulting job loss are part of his own "soul's plan" for personal growth in this lifetime. You certainly

59

didn't intend for anyone to get hurt when you performed your job-getting spell.

Nonetheless, there might be a connection here, since the cook could have easily ended up working through his karmic lesson in some other way that didn't involve losing a job.

Again, this is an extreme example, but it shows how unintended consequences can arise from magical work when we are not careful. If you always remember to use "for the good of all and harm to none" with your spellwork, you can be assured that you won't inadvertently cause trouble for others.

As busy people in a modern culture that often prizes convenience and speed above all else, it can be easy to make the mistake of deciding that our spells haven't worked if we don't see immediate results. It's important to recognize that magic has its own process and its own timing, which may or may not align with our wishes.

If a spell doesn't seem to be working, there could be many reasons.

It's possible that there just isn't a way for what you want to manifest at this time in a way that is for the good of all and harms no one. Sometimes we work spells for things we're not actually ready for ourselves, such as love relationships or new homes.

Spells can take varying lengths of time to come to fruition—it can sometimes be the case that by the time the manifestation occurs, the spell has long been forgotten by the person who cast it. You can also inadvertently "cancel" the power of your magic by being filled with doubt about whether or not the spell worked. If you begin doubting, you are sending the Universe a message saying "never mind about that spell, I didn't mean it."

It's always important, then, to maintain trust in right timing when it comes to magic.

However, if you feel certain, after three weeks of nothing happening, that your magic didn't work, you may want to try again, with more confidence and better focus. Or you might try a different spell. Don't feel like a failure if your first attempt (or even second and third!) doesn't pan out. In addition to correct intention and timing, magic takes practice. The next section of this guide will provide plenty of ideas for you to try as you begin your practice of the art of candle magic.

PART THREE

CANDLE
MAGIC SPELLS

GETTING STARTED

Below are several spells for help in matters of love, employment, money, health, and other important contributors to an enjoyable life. Each has one or more candles as its focus, with some involving a few more ingredients, most of which should be readily available.

As mentioned above, if you have trouble acquiring any of the essential oils, you can make your own magical blend with ingredients from your kitchen. A few recipes for homemade oils can be found at the end of the spells section.

More importantly, please remember that you can tailor any of these spells to your own needs—it's your ability to focus your intentions through your own personal power that truly makes the difference.

You'll notice that for each spell, the ideal Moon phase and day of the week for working this type of magic are listed.

Generally, the waxing phase of the Moon is for magic that attracts things into your life, while the waning phase is for releasing old or unwanted things from your life.

Likewise the days of the week have traditional magical associations. Friday, for example, is recommended for spells involving love, friendship, reconciliation, and beauty. It's okay if you can't time your spellwork exactly to these recommendations, but doing so is very likely to boost the power of the spell.

Finally, be sure to take some time to prepare yourself for magic, rather than robotically going through the motions as if you were folding laundry or preparing the lunch you'll be taking to work tomorrow. Whether you prefer to cast a circle, meditate, and/or utilize other methods for "attuning" to the unseen realms, doing something to mark a distinction between magic time and the rest of your day will ensure that you're in the right frame of mind to have an impact.

LOVE SPELLS

Matters of the heart are probably the most common reason that people seek out magic.

It's understandable to want to do whatever it takes to bring love into one's life. However, there are a lot of irresponsible spells out there, claiming to be able to "win" you the person you desire.

Spells that aim to manipulate someone else, no matter how ultimately well-intentioned, are not responsible magic, and are very likely to backfire. So it's important that you focus on the *situation* you desire, rather than the *person*, when working these spells.

After all, you never know what's around the corner— the person you have a crush on today may pale in comparison to someone you're about to meet next week!

MOONLIGHT LOVE ATTRACTION SPELL

For singles wanting to enjoy the dating scene, here's a simple spell to heighten your ability to attract potential suitors. This is particularly good for those who have been single for a long time and may struggle to remain optimistic about their prospects.

Moon phase: Waxing
Ideal day: Friday

You will need:

- 1 Pink candle (spell candle sized)
- Small vial of wearable essential oil blend (or cologne/perfume if preferred)
- Cinnamon, jasmine, or lavender incense
- Crystal point, athame, or other ritual carving tool

Instructions:

Light the incense.

Using the crystal point or other carving tool, carve a heart in the center of the candle.

Place the candle in a window, ideally one with a direct view of the Moon. (If this isn't possible, visualize the moon as you set the candle down.) Place the vial in front of candle so that it stands between the candle and the window.

Take a few moments to call up the feelings of well-being, excitement, and companionship. Hold this feeling as you get ready to light the candle. As you light it, say these (or your own) words:

By this moon's light, let love shine bright.

Allow it to burn all the way down. Wear the oil (or perfume) when you go out to help you stay confident in your ability to attract new love. But be careful not to overdo the scent—that never helps!

FINDING YOUR
IDEAL PARTNER SPELL

For those who are ready to move beyond casual dating and want assistance in manifesting a solid, healthy relationship.

This spell asks you to identify what you're truly looking for in a partner, so spend some time considering this beforehand.

As an added "boost," you can consult color meanings and choose a candle color that aligns with the qualities you feel are most important in a partner. For example, if you know that sharp intelligence and ability with language are key, you might choose a yellow candle. If no colors or qualities jump out at you as being at the top of the list, then feel free to use a white candle.

Moon phase: Waxing
Ideal day: Friday

<u>You will need:</u>

- A pen and a piece of white paper
- 1 small candle (white, or color of your choice)
- 1 gold or silver ribbon, long enough to wrap around your palm at least twice

Instructions:

Light the candle, and wrap the ribbon around your non-writing hand.

On the paper, write down the specific things you desire in a partner for a long-term relationship. Spend a good while on this part. Be sure to include how you want to feel around and be treated by this person, as all the desirable characteristics in the world won't matter if you're being ignored or abused in any way.

Fold the paper into a small square, then unwrap the ribbon from your hand and tie it around the folded paper.

Hold the bundle together in your palms as you meditate on how you will feel in this relationship once it is underway.

Place the bundle under your mattress for one week, then bury in a potted plant or in the yard.

SPICE UP YOUR RELATIONSHIP SPELL

Those of us already in long-term relationships may sometimes long wistfully for the rush of feelings that accompanies the beginning of a romance.

While you can't turn back the clock to your relationship's early days, you can rejuvenate the atmosphere between you and your partner with this simple spell.

This can be done during any point in the Moon's cycle—if you're working during the waning phase, focus on ridding the relationship of any "humdrum" feelings or stagnant-seeming energy.

Moon phase: Any
Ideal day: Tuesday or Friday

You will need:

- 2 red votive candles
- Plate to melt them on
- Jasmine oil (or homemade blend)
- Pinch of rosemary (fresh or dried)

Instructions:

Anoint the candles with the oil and stand them next to each other on the plate.

Sprinkle the rosemary on top of the candles and in a circle around them.

Say:

As these flames dance side by side, so we two renew our stride, in love and in desire.

It's ideal to let the candles burn out in one sitting, but it's also fine to snuff them out and repeat the spell the next night, if necessary.

Once they're all the way gone, take some time to look at the melted wax and see if any impressions or messages about your relationship emerge.

MONEY SPELLS

Many skeptics of magic will ask, "If it works so well, why don't people just cast spells to win the lottery?"

If only it were this simple.

Magic works in cooperation with physical reality, which means the mathematical odds are still in play. You're also competing with the wishes and dreams of many, many people—and whether they're working spells or not, their intentions do factor in.

Furthermore, winning money may not be in your best interest in the grand scheme of things—just look at all the tales of woe among those who strike it rich unexpectedly.

Wiccans and other Witches know that we have to do our part in manifesting wealth—by working, making smart decisions about our money, etc.

As you develop your magical abilities, be sure to acknowledge and express gratitude for all gifts from the Universe—even for the penny you find on the sidewalk.

Let no luck be too small—otherwise, the spirit realm may interpret your attitude to mean you're not really interested in experiencing good luck!

QUICK "POCKET CHANGE" MONEY SPELL

This is a great spell for beginners, as it can have immediate and surprising results—even if it doesn't impact your life in a major way.

Stay relaxed and open to the possibility of money coming in from unexpected sources, and enjoy the magic!

Moon phase: Waxing
Ideal day: Thursday

You will need:

- 1 green spell candle
- 1 coin big enough to set the candle on
- Crystal point, athame, or other ritual carving tool

Instructions:

Carve a dollar sign, or the sign of your own currency, into the candle. Hold it in your hands for a few moments & repeat these (or your own) words three times:

As like attracts like, this money brings more.

Light the candle and allow it to burn down to the coin.

Carry the coin with you in your purse, wallet, or the pocket of some item of clothing that you wear daily.

RENT AND BILLS STABILITY—7 DAY SPELL

If you often end up scraping to get the bills paid, or are in a transition period and unsure of how your finances are going to work out in the near future, this is a good spell to aid you in establishing some peace of mind about staying afloat.

Once you've sent this spell energy out into the spirit world, you can focus on manifesting more long-term improvements to your financial life.

Moon phase: Waxing
Ideal day: Thursday or Sunday

You will need:

- 1 check from your checkbook (or piece of paper)
- 1 7-day candle, preferably gold, grey, brown, or orange
- A pinch of basil
- Almond, patchouli, or bergamot oil

Instructions:

Anoint the top of the candle with one or two drops of the oil. Sprinkle the basil over the oil.

Focus on the feeling of ease that comes with having everything in order financially.

Light the candle as you say:

All is provided to me exactly as I need it, with harm to none. So let it be.

Sit with the candlelight for a few moments and write some positive affirmations about money and stability on the check or piece of paper. Be sure to write as if the magic has already worked—for example, you might write "All bills are paid and I can move forward with confidence."

Make sure you use words that resonate with you and help you strengthen your belief in your ability to manifest positive change.

Fold the check (or paper) into thirds, then keep folding until it's as small as you can make it.

Place it in your purse or wallet and carry it with you until your bills are paid.

Leave the candle to burn out on its own. This typically takes 7 days, though if things are manifesting at a more rapid rate, the candle may burn out more quickly.

BANISHING
MONEY BLOCKS SPELL

Many people have unconscious attitudes about money that prevent them from ever getting what they desire.

We may say we want a bigger salary, or more in our savings account, etc., but when we look at our circumstances we conclude that it's impossible, since we can't see any solutions. Or we may think that wanting money at all is a sign of greed that goes against our better, "spiritual" natures.

Unlike most money-related spells, this one is done during a waning Moon, as it focuses on releasing these unhelpful, and often unconscious, attitudes and fears.

If you've been unsuccessful at other spellwork to attract money, you might want to give this one a try—it could be that you've been unknowingly getting in your own way!

Moon phase: Waning
Ideal day: Thursday, Sunday, or Monday

You will need:

- 1 black candle
- 1 piece of white paper
- Scissors
- Cauldron, sink. or other safe place to burn paper

Instructions:

Light the candle and sit quietly for a few moments.

On the paper, write down your fears about money. Go with the first few things that pop into your mind—these are usually the thoughts that block our progress toward prosperity.

Name each fear in a simple, single sentence. Leave space in between each sentence so that you can cut them into strips.

Cut the first "money fears" sentence from the top of the paper. Read it silently, and then speak its opposite out loud. For example, if you've written "I will never have enough," then say, "I always have more than enough."

Then light the paper on the candle and allow it to burn out in your cauldron, sink, or other fire-proof container.

Gently snuff or wave out the candle.

Repeat this spell each night, burning one fear sentence per night, until you've burned them all. The ideal length for this spell is 3 to 5 consecutive nights.

EMPLOYMENT SPELLS

Job hunting can be stressful even in the best of times, but it can also be exciting if we stay open to unseen possibilities.

These spells can boost your power during this time of reckoning with the unknown!

LUCKY JOB SEARCH SPELL

This very simple spell is great for those who tend to get anxious about whether or not a spell is working, as you have multiple chances to repeat it—though you shouldn't need very many!

Start this on a Sunday, which is the day associated with work and career matters.

Moon phase: Any
Ideal day: Sundays

<u>**You will need:**</u>

- 1 gold or yellow candle

<u>**Instructions:**</u>

Light the candle as you say these or your own words:

I am joyfully and gainfully employed, and filled with gratitude.

Spend a few moments imagining the feelings of relief and excitement that come after being hired for a job you know you will enjoy.

Let the candle burn for eight minutes (or longer, if you wish) as you visualize the feeling of working in a job that you find exciting and well-paying, then snuff it out gently.

Repeat the spell each Sunday until the candle has burned down completely, or until you find a job—whichever comes first.

EMPLOYMENT VICTORY SPELL

So you've applied for a job you want—now what?

Boost your confidence—and therefore your chances of landing it—with this spell.

If you work this spell during a waxing Moon, focus your visualization on beginning the job. If you work it during a waning Moon, focus on winnowing away the competition from other applicants so that you emerge victorious.

Be careful here, though, to do it *for the good of all and harm to none*, rather than focusing on causing disappointment for others!

Moon phase: Any
Ideal day: Tuesday

<u>You will need:</u>

- 1 green candle
- 1 orange candle
- Crystal point, athame, or other ritual carving tool

<u>Instructions:</u>

On the orange candle, carve a "V" for victory.

On the green candle, carve an "F" for fortune.

Stand them as close together as possible, and light the orange candle, then the green.

As they burn, repeat this mantra for at least three minutes:

With this fire divine, the job is mine.

This spell works best if the candles burn down in a single night, but you can repeat it on successive nights until the candle is gone, if necessary.

HEALING SPELLS

We know that, like anything else, the body is essentially made of energy. Many popular alternative healing modalities make use of this understanding, such as reiki, quigong, and therapeutic touch.

With this in mind, it makes perfect sense that magic can positively affect our health.

However, you should *never* substitute magic for actual medical care!

As with any other "alternative" practice, magic should be used *in addition to*, not instead of, any necessary medical interventions. Just as in money or employment matters, you're expected to do your part to manifest the change you seek.

These spells can work well during any phase of the moon, since any healing involves both sending away disease (imbalance) and attracting health (balance).

SIMPLE HEALING SPELL

For everyday ailments such as the common cold, or more chronic issues such as arthritis flare-ups, this spell gently supports the body's natural healing abilities.

It can be worked all at once or over a series of days, depending on the nature of the imbalance you're seeking to heal and your general preferences. If you choose to work it over more than one night, be sure to use a new pinch of yarrow each time.

Moon phase: Any
Ideal day: Sunday or Monday

<u>You will need:</u>

- 1 blue candle
- A pinch of dried yarrow

<u>Instructions:</u>

Light the candle.

Close your eyes and visualize white light filling and surrounding the part of you that needs healing (for example, if you're dealing with a bronchial infection, focus on the lungs).

Once you have this image firmly in your mind, then visualize the white light growing and expending until it surrounds your entire being.

Hold this image for a few moments and notice the shift in your body as you mentally flood it with light.

When you're ready, open your eyes and sprinkle a small bit of yarrow into the flame.

Thank the Universe for its healing powers and close the ritual with words of confirmation, such as:

For the good of all and harm to none, this magical healing work is done.

If you aren't leaving the candle to burn out completely, wait at least 15 minutes before snuffing it out.

HEALING SPELL
FOR LOVED ONES

It can be a wonderful experience to work healing magic for others, rather than for yourself.

However, if you're going to do spellwork for someone else, it's strongly recommended that you get permission first. (If you're not able to be fully open about your magical life, you could just ask the person if they'd be comfortable with you praying for them. Magic is, after all, a powerful kind of prayer.)

In addition, if you're troubled by worries about this person, do some work to release those feelings before working the spell, so that you don't cloud up the message you're sending to the spirit realm!

Moon phase: Any
Ideal day: Sunday or Monday

<u>You will need:</u>

- 1 white candle
- Eucalyptus or lavender oil
- Crystal point, athame, or other ritual carving tool

<u>Instructions:</u>

Carve the name of the person you're working the spell for into the candle, beginning at the base and working toward the top.

Anoint the candle with a few drops of the oil, starting at the bottom and working up to the middle, then starting from the top and working back down to the middle.

As you prepare the candle, focus your mind on a vision of your friend or loved one glowing radiantly in good health.

When you feel ready, light the candle and say the following words, or use words of your own:

> *Bright light, this healing white surrounds and makes [name of person] new.*

If at all possible, leave the candle to burn all the way down on its own.

BANISHING DEPRESSION SPELL

Depression is often described by those who suffer from it as an unwanted presence in the mind that turns every thought into a sour, mucky experience.

It can be very challenging to make use of positive imagery when under the "spell" of depression, so it's helpful to first do some work toward banishing the negative influences underlying this harmful condition.

Because the focus here is on banishing, the spell is most powerful during a waning moon, but don't let that prevent you from using magic to take care of yourself—it can still be done at any time!

Moon phase: Any (waning is ideal)
Ideal day: Saturday, Sunday, Monday, or Wednesday

You will need:

- 1 black candle (preferably with a shorter burning time)
- 3 white candles
- 1 small black crystal or stone (such as obsidian, black tourmaline, or jet)
- 1 piece quartz crystal (or other white stone)
- Small black cloth

Instructions:

Arrange the white candles in a triangle, and place the black candle in the center.

Hold the black stone between your palms and spend a few moments directing all negative energy from your body and mind into the stone. When you feel ready, place the stone next to the black candle and light it.

Say the following words, or use your own:

I release and banish all negativity from my being.

Next, hold the quartz crystal (or other white stone) between your palms and focus on pulling in healing, loving energy from the Universe. Visualize your entire body flooded with, and surrounded by, white light.

When you feel ready, light the white candles, repeating this mantra as you light each one:

I welcome and trust all positivity and Universal love into my being.

Once the black candle has burned all the way down, discard any remaining wax, and clean the candle holder before putting it away.

Use the black cloth to pick up the black stone so that you avoid touching it with your skin. If possible, toss the stone in a moving body of water, such as a stream, river, or ocean. If this isn't possible, bury it somewhere away from your home.

Keep the quartz crystal (or white stone) in your pocket or in a pouch that you keep near you at all times. You may also want to keep it near your bed while you sleep.

You can snuff out and relight the white candles as much as you wish—they can be very comforting as you continue to heal from the depression. Just be sure to use all three of them until they are completely gone.

MORE SPELLS FOR LIFE ENHANCEMENT

Here are a few more spells for tackling life's challenges and making the most of the opportunities that come your way.

COURAGE SPELL

This spell can help you approach any daunting task, whether it's a job interview, a medical procedure, or something more pleasant but still nerve-wracking, like a first date.

Its ideal day is Tuesday—the day associated with Mars, which gives it its association with matters of courage—but don't let that stop you from working this spell on any day you need to!

Moon phase: Waxing
Ideal day: Tuesday

You will need:

- 4 orange candles
- Clove oil (optional)
- 1 small object to "charm" (such as a crystal or other stone, a small piece of jewelry, or other small personal item)

Instructions:

Anoint the candles (if using oil), and arrange them in a square pattern. Place the crystal or other object in the center of the square.

Spend a few moments identifying a situation in which you have felt truly confident and courageous—you may want to do some brainstorming on paper to "dig up" a really solid memory.

Once you've got a visual, focus on it with all of your attention for a few moments. You are going to infuse the object you've placed in the square of candles with this powerful courage, so that you can draw from it later when you need to feel it again.

Light the candles, repeating this mantra as you light each one:

This fire of courage burns always in my heart.

Allow the candles to burn down, then keep your courage charm in your pocket (or wear it, if it's jewelry) whenever you need an extra boost of confidence.

GOOD LUCK SPELL

Nearly everyone has had what many call a "bad luck streak," when things just seem to go constantly wrong.

It doesn't help that our mainstream culture tends to reinforce a belief in these bad luck streaks, while eyeing "good luck streaks" somewhat suspiciously. (The phrase "I can't believe my luck!" usually refers to good things happening, as opposed to unfortunate things.)

This spell boosts your ability to attract good luck by counteracting negative thought patterns around luck and fortune.

Moon phase: Any
Ideal day: Thursday or Sunday

You will need:

- 1 black candle
- 1 white candle
- 1 green candle
- Pinch of chamomile and/or star anise

Instructions:

Arrange the candles side-by-side with the white one in the middle.

Sprinkle the herb(s) in a circle around the candles.

Light the black candle and say, *All bad luck away.*

Then light the green candle and say, *All good luck to stay.*

Finally, say, *Open my eyes and my ears to good fortune,* and then light the white candle.

Send out your intention to be more aware of *everything* that goes right in your life, no matter how seemingly trivial.

Try working this spell once a week for four weeks, and take notes during this time about what you observe. Record all the positive things that happen to you, and do NOT record any negative things. This is about retraining the brain to focus more consistently on the positive, so don't muddy up the work by including any details that don't support your vision of a lucky and charmed life.

When you repeat the spell, have your notes with you and spend a few moments in gratitude for what you have recently noticed regarding good luck in your life.

HELPFUL ANSWERS SPELL

For those big, burning questions that just won't leave you alone.

While it's often true that we can't know the answer to a question until we're absolutely meant to, you can ask the Universe to send you helpful information along the way. Just be sure you're open to whatever the answer might be—if you're too attached to a certain outcome, you might not be able to "hear" the truth when the spirit realm whispers it to you.

The answers may come in a dream, or in a moment of synchronicity in your waking life, such as a phrase spoken in a conversation with a friend or acquaintance.

Moon phase: Waning, particularly just before the New Moon
Ideal day: Monday or Wednesday

You will need:

- 1 yellow or gold candle
- 1 strip of paper, long enough to write your question on
- Crystal point, athame, or other ritual carving tool

Instructions:

Think clearly about your question and write it as concisely as possible on the strip of paper.

Carve one to three words that represent the question into the candle, starting at the bottom and working up to the tip.

Light the candle, and burn the strip of paper.

Allow the candle to burn down.

You should receive an answer within 7 days.

PSYCHIC ATTACK
REVERSAL SPELL

Many resources on magic mention psychic attack, but unless you know other people in your life who a) practice magic and b) would actually work magic to hurt you in some way, you're unlikely to become a victim of an overt magical attack.

However, because thought is energy, it's definitely possible to be undermined by the negative thoughts of others—particularly those who may be resentful or envious of us for whatever reason.

These thoughts are also a form of psychic attack, even if the perpetrator doesn't intentionally mean harm against us. This spell helps you eliminate any effects of the negative thoughts and feelings of others.

Moon phase: Waning
Ideal day: Tuesday or Saturday

You will need:

- 1 black candle
- 5 garlic cloves
- 1 teaspoon honey

Instructions:

Arrange the garlic cloves around the black candle in the shape of a five-pointed star. Visualize the garlic absorbing any and all negative energy in and around your body.

When you're ready, say:

I release any and all negativity.
I am protected from all harmful thought from all directions.
I am healed from any harmful effects of the thoughts of others.

Light the candle, and eat the honey.

When the spell is done, bury the garlic cloves outside.

A WITCH'S CRAFT

These days, Wicca and Witchcraft have become more popular than at any point in history.

You can find an incredible range of resources on the Internet and in print, as well as countless magical products for sale, including magical blends of oils, herbs, and pre-charged candles.

Although many of these products undoubtedly work quite well, you don't have to buy everything you need for successful magic—you can make many magical tools and ingredients all on your own.

The "DIY" approach is not only potentially less expensive, but allows you to add your own magical energy to whatever you create for use in spellwork.

OILS

For some people, essential oils can seem to present a barrier to successful spellwork, as they can be difficult to find and/or cost-prohibitive.

However, you can make your own herb-infused oils with common kitchen ingredients that can work just as well as any store-bought blend—all you need is a base oil, such as olive, almond, or safflower, and a handful or two of your favorite herbs.

To make your own magical oils, try this simple recipe:

- 1 part herb(s)
- 2 parts oil
- Mason jar (or other jar with a tight-fitting lid)
- Cheesecloth (optional)

Instructions:

Pour the oil into the jar, then add the herbs.

For best results, focus your intention on the purpose of the oil, whether it's for love, money, or just strengthening magical power in general as you do so.

Close the jar tightly, and leave in a cool, dark place for three to five days. You can then strain the oil through a cheesecloth into another jar. This step isn't strictly necessary, though it will help the oil to keep longer if the herbs themselves are removed.

Use your oil to anoint your candles, and even your skin as a preparation for magic!

Here are a few herb combinations to try:

- **Prosperity:** alfalfa, bay leaf, basil
- **Healing:** thyme, rosemary, goldenseal
- **Love:** cardamom, cinnamon, hibiscus
- **All-purpose magic booster:** anise seed, basil, rosemary

CANDLES AND HOLDERS

It's hard to imagine now, but candles were actually not widely available for purchase until the 19th century. This meant that most people made their own—including Witches.

You can create powerful spellwork by making your own candles, and plenty of recipes for beeswax and soy candles can be found online. Some stores even sell sheets of beeswax for quick and easy candle-making!

If making candles is a little too labor-intensive, you can still take a DIY approach to your candle magic through the art of "repurposing."

7-day novena candles, which are widely available, even in grocery stores these days, can be turned into deity or Element candles, according to your own tradition.

You can paint these or other jar candles with colors, designs, and/or images that represent the God, the Goddess, and/or Element(s) you wish to honor with the candle.

Struggling to acquire all those different sizes and shapes of candle holders for various types of candles? Try painting the base of a clay pot with a pentacle or other magical symbol for a unique ritual tool.

Magic is about creativity, so use your own when and where you can!

CONCLUSION

This guide should provide you with everything you need to start practicing candle magic—now it's time to start practicing your spellwork!

Following the spells included in this book will get you started, but as your confidence grows I highly recommend you start experimenting and creating your own spells as you learn to deepen your intuition and psychic awareness.

Remember that learning occurs as you go, and that it takes time to achieve proficiency in magic, as it does with any other skill. To that end, you'll find resources for further reading listed below, as well as Tables of Correspondence to refer to when substituting ingredients or creating your own spells.

Whether you consider yourself to be Wiccan, a Witch, or you're just curious, I have tried to make this guide as accessible as possible to anyone with an interest.

As I've reiterated throughout this guide, when it comes to Wicca, there is no right or wrong. Other resources may differ in their explanations and meanings to this guide, and that's fine by me! You'll find your own way on your Wiccan journey, and the most important thing is to hold onto the ideas, meanings, and beliefs that resonate with *you*. If you're a relative beginner, having something to follow to get you started—like this guide—should prove helpful, but as you develop you will most likely find your own path.

Everything I have included in this book are my personal interpretations of the topic at hand, and the way I understand things may differ from other authors, which may differ from you—this is one of the reasons I find talking to other Wiccans so fascinating!

However, one thing will ring true for all Wiccans: keep your intentions positive and clear. Magic can positively impact your life, but you should never use it to seek gain at the expense of others.

Before practicing any type of magic, I would always encourage you to think about how your action could impact others. For example, a love spell aimed at one person—while coming from an inherently good place—is trying to force someone to act against their will. Even if you think you're acting in that person's best interest, it's not your decision to make.

Understand this and the results of magic can be a really strong addition to your life.

I will leave you with that thought, as it is now time for you to continue your own journey, and to begin practicing some of the techniques outlined in this book.

If you aren't seeing results immediately, don't get too frustrated. Keep practicing, keep putting your positive intentions out into the Universe, and it will happen.

I sincerely hoped you enjoyed learning about candle magic with me, as it is a topic close to my heart. I wish you all the best on your magical adventures, and hope it is a wonderful addition to your life!

Thank you one more time for reading.

Blessed Be.

TABLES OF CORRESPONDENCE

Included here are very brief sample tables of correspondence. You can consult these when exploring options for ritual, spellwork, and other Craft activity.

Be sure to research further, however—there are countless tables of correspondence with much more detailed information than is presented in this brief guide.

TABLE ONE: HERBS

Herb	General Magical Use
Basil	fosters loving vibrations, protection, wards off negativities in a home
Chamomile	brings love, healing, relieves stressful situations
Cinnamon	love, luck, prosperity, success, raises spiritual vibrations
Hibiscus	divinations, dreams, love and lust
Mugwort	psychic powers, protection, increases lust and fertility—**do not ingest, and do not handle if pregnant**
Rosemary	love and lust spells, promotes healthy rest
Star Anise	luck, spiritual connection, psychic and magical power
Thyme	attracts loyalty, affection, psychic abilities
Valerian	protection, drives away negativity, purifies sacred space
Yarrow	healing, divination, love, promotes courage and confidence

TABLE TWO: ESSENTIAL OILS

Essential Oil	General Magical Use
Bergamot	promotes energy, success, prosperity
Cinnamon	increases psychic connections, promotes healing, success, luck
Clove	protection, courage, banishing negative energies, cleanses auras
Eucalyptus	healing and purification
Frankincense	relieves stress, aids meditation, brings heightened spiritual awareness
Jasmine	strengthens intuition and inspiration, promotes sensuality and love
Lavender	healing, cleansing, removing anxiety
Patchouli	prosperity, lust, physical energy
Sandalwood	clears negativity, promotes balanced energy flow
Ylang-Ylang	promotes happiness, calms anger, enhances sexual attraction

TABLE THREE:
DAYS OF THE WEEK

Day	Magical Influences
Sunday	healing, protection, business and career success, spirituality
Monday	home and family matters, peace, healing, psychic awareness
Tuesday	passion, competition, protection, strength, lust, courage
Wednesday	inspiration, study, wisdom, divination, understanding
Thursday	money, prosperity, success, material gain, generosity
Friday	love, friendship, comfort, arts, beauty, reconciliation
Saturday	long-term projects, wisdom, karmic lessons, endings

SUGGESTIONS FOR FURTHER READING

Note: You may find that some of the information in these books differs from what's detailed in this guide. This is due to the wide variety of magical traditions and practices, and is also part of what makes magic so enjoyable—the ability to blend your own intuition with time-tested knowledge. As with anything else in Witchcraft, take what makes sense to you, and disregard what doesn't. Happy reading!

Kardia Zoe, *Wicca: A Beginner's Guide to Casting Spells: Herbal, Crystal and Candle Magic* (2015)

Raymond Buckland, *Practical Candleburning Rituals* (1982)

D.J. Conway, *A Little Book of Candle Magic* (2000)

Phillip Cooper, *Candle Magic: A Coveted Collection of Spells, Rituals, and Magical Paradigms* (2000)

Charmaine Day, *The Magic Candle: Facts and Fundamentals of Ritual Candle-Burning* (1982)

Ember Grant, *Magical Candle Crafting* (2011)

THREE FREE
AUDIOBOOKS PROMOTION

Don't forget, you can now enjoy **three audiobooks completely free of charge** when you start a free 30-day trial with Audible.

If you're new to the Craft, *Wicca Starter Kit* contains three of Lisa's most popular books for beginning Wiccans. You can download it for free at:

www.wiccaliving.com/free-wiccan-audiobooks

Or, if you're wanting to expand your magical skills, check out *Spellbook Starter Kit,* with three collections of spellwork featuring the powerful energies of candles, colors, crystals, mineral stones, and magical herbs. Download over 150 spells for free at:

www.wiccaliving.com/free-spell-audiobooks

Members receive free audiobooks every month, as well as exclusive discounts. And, if you don't want to continue with Audible, just remember to cancel your membership. You won't be charged a cent, and you'll get to keep your books!

Happy listening!

MORE BOOKS BY LISA CHAMBERLAIN

Wicca for Beginners: A Guide to Wiccan Beliefs, Rituals, Magic, and Witchcraft

Wicca Book of Spells: A Book of Shadows for Wiccans, Witches, and Other Practitioners of Magic

Wicca Herbal Magic: A Beginner's Guide to Practicing Wiccan Herbal Magic, with Simple Herb Spells

Wicca Book of Herbal Spells: A Book of Shadows for Wiccans, Witches, and Other Practitioners of Herbal Magic

Wicca Candle Magic: A Beginner's Guide to Practicing Wiccan Candle Magic, with Simple Candle Spells

Wicca Book of Candle Spells: A Book of Shadows for Wiccans, Witches, and Other Practitioners of Candle Magic

Wicca Crystal Magic: A Beginner's Guide to Practicing Wiccan Crystal Magic, with Simple Crystal Spells

Wicca Book of Crystal Spells: A Book of Shadows for Wiccans, Witches, and Other Practitioners of Crystal Magic

Tarot for Beginners: A Guide to Psychic Tarot Reading, Real Tarot Card Meanings, and Simple Tarot Spreads

Runes for Beginners: A Guide to Reading Runes in Divination, Rune Magic, and the Meaning of the Elder Futhark Runes

Wicca Moon Magic: A Wiccan's Guide and Grimoire for Working Magic with Lunar Energies

Wicca Wheel of the Year Magic: A Beginner's Guide to the Sabbats, with History, Symbolism, Celebration Ideas, and Dedicated Sabbat Spells

Wicca Kitchen Witchery: A Beginner's Guide to Magical Cooking, with Simple Spells and Recipes

Wicca Essential Oils Magic: A Beginner's Guide to Working with Magical Oils, with Simple Recipes and Spells

Wicca Elemental Magic: A Guide to the Elements, Witchcraft, and Magical Spells

Wicca Magical Deities: A Guide to the Wiccan God and Goddess, and Choosing a Deity to Work Magic With

Wicca Living a Magical Life: A Guide to Initiation and Navigating Your Journey in the Craft

Magic and the Law of Attraction: A Witch's Guide to the Magic of Intention, Raising Your Frequency, and Building Your Reality

Wicca Altar and Tools: A Beginner's Guide to Wiccan Altars, Tools for Spellwork, and Casting the Circle

Wicca Finding Your Path: A Beginner's Guide to Wiccan Traditions, Solitary Practitioners, Eclectic Witches, Covens, and Circles

Wicca Book of Shadows: A Beginner's Guide to Keeping Your Own Book of Shadows and the History of Grimoires

Modern Witchcraft and Magic for Beginners: A Guide to Traditional and Contemporary Paths, with Magical Techniques for the Beginner Witch

FREE GIFT REMINDER

Just a reminder that Lisa is giving away an exclusive, free spell book as a thank-you gift to new readers!

Little Book of Spells contains ten spells that are ideal for newcomers to the practice of magic, but are also suitable for any level of experience.

Read it on read on your laptop, phone, tablet, Kindle or Nook device by visiting:

www.wiccaliving.com/bonus

DID YOU ENJOY
WICCA CANDLE MAGIC?

Thanks so much for reading this book! I know there are many great books out there about Wicca, so I really appreciate you choosing this one.

If you enjoyed the book, I have a small favor to ask— would you take a couple of minutes to leave a review for this book on Amazon?

Your feedback will help me to make improvements to this book, and to create even better ones in the future. It will also help me develop new ideas for books on other topics that might be of interest to you. Thanks in advance for your help!

Made in the USA
Monee, IL
03 February 2021